M000024481

BROTHER BULLET

Volume 84

Sun Tracks

An American Indian Literary Series

CASANDRA LÓPEZ

BROTHER BULLET

poems

THE UNIVERSITY OF
ARIZONA PRESS
TUCSON

The University of Arizona Press
www.uapress.arizona.edu

ISBN-13: 978-0-8165-3852-2 (paper)

Cover design by Leigh McDonald
Cover photo by Mercedes Dorame. *Ascension - Pakook*, 2013.

Publication of this book is made possible in part by the proceeds of a permanent endowment cre-
ated with the assistance of a Challenge Grant from the National Endowment for the Humanities,
a federal agency.

Library of Congress Cataloging-in-Publication Data
Names: López, Casandra, author.
Title: Brother Bullet : poems / Casandra López.
Other titles: Sun tracks ; v. 84.
Description: Tucson : The University of Arizona Press, 2019. | Series: Sun tracks : an American
    Indian literary series ; volume 84
Identifiers: LCCN 2018026817 | ISBN 9780816538522 (pbk. : alk. paper)
Subjects: LCSH: López, Casandra—Family—Poetry. | Murder—Poetry. | LCGFT: Poetry.
Classification: LCC PS3612.O584 A6 2019 | DDC 811/.6—dc23 LC record available at https://
    lccn.loc.gov/2018026817

Printed in the United States of America
♾ This paper meets the requirements of ANSI/NISO Z39.48-1992 (Permanence of Paper).

CONTENTS

BROTHER BULLET

BULLET BREAKS

WHERE BULLET BREAKS

San Bernardino 2010

Come—
See where Bullet broke
Brother, see where I break,
where we split into before
and after. We fracture
                    at the root, both
                              believers in science and prayer.

But first,
there is childhood home. There is porch,
and twinned doors. 18 panes
of glass. Something
always being
                    broken, by a ball, a falling
                              broom, scuffling
                                        and break-dancing boys.

Bodies spin, on hardwood. Bone
and tendon twist. They are breakers.
See their hands touching chest—touching
heart, back and forth.   Rush
                    of hot breath. They coil like DNA.

                    Were we ever that alive?

Sky-blue
door replaces glass. Even
before Bullet, those muscled days
seemed long ago, as years grew
into the steady rhythm of family.

Until   that   night.
    Come,
       there is so much   noise,
so much   darkness,   voices
      collide. Bullet steals   the beat,
takes   thigh, chest, and brain
      of Brother. Steals   my   breath.
My Bullet   is in   the sky
     blue door,   in the metal,
  in a moment.   It hangs there,
     that hook   in me,   to you.

10TH ST PORCH

Investigation

Outline us in yellow tape, label us: Investigation.
Witness 1. Witness 2. Photograph the blood, chair, blue door, photograph

the fear. After the police left, Father washed
your blood from concrete, the porch you once painted baby

blue, peeled to gray, to ochre red streams. Father hosed the porch, irrigated—
blood until it swam into the dampened

dirt, into the bushes and bird of paradise. The cream orchid and spiny aloe vera
drowned from all those days of rain, that drummed and

drummed into the roof of our mouths—
we felt so liquid. We longed for dryness, for explanation.

But Bullet stained us somber. Catalogue our cries, mark us blind—
we can only see gray, your gasping mouth.

Mark us as prey, mark us tainted and blood stained—we are so lost in the veil
of rain. We hid the bullet hole in the door beneath a Christmas wreath,

candles lit—St. Jude and the Just Judge, inches
from where Bullet ripped into you quick, downing you

to the cracked cement, prayers in the mist. Even now we are still
not dry, our insides remain

dank with ghost. Blood feeds soil, evaporates. Techs come looking for shell
casings. The porch is a beach, metal detectors

in hand they wait for pings, wait
for some kind of sign. Between us, and them—an ocean. We do not speak

to each other, we know something is missing. Your body, your
belly that was once a warm wave, where your Daughter drifted to sleep.

FATHER MADE US

Out of orange groves, from canyon
blood, so we may thrive—
in this desert.

Brother, what am I without you? Half
of something we didn't know

was whole. We still tend the trees, like grandfather
taught us, eat our oranges, fingernail
our way into the rinds, into the bitter.

Our lemons taste sweet, or maybe it's longing
that makes it so.

Your Daughter squeezes them
on everything she eats, learns to savor each
sour golden bud with such devotion.

I remember the way you looked at each child:
a satellite's gaze.

Brother, what did you father in her? What can be fathered
in nine years, or six, or even three months?
Will Baby remember your cradle arm?

I COULD HAVE

Pushed past gauze and reached my hand into
your chest, past skin just surgeoned skin flapped

open, and held your heart in my palm, until

my arms weakened, and gave out. I've held birds in my palms,
our clipped dove and Great Grandmother's bright plumed finches,

such lightness frantic for flight. Is this what your heart would have felt like?

I wanted to ask the doctor to split you open, cleave a little further,
from clavicle to twin hipped pelvis, so I could crawl inside.

I could have blown into your lungs,

snapped my fingertips at your synapses. Instead, I touched your
bloated hand. Spread out before us, still, but not death still,

machines beeped, brain activity— — —antiseptic rustling. Body began
to swell and purple; face turning into a horrible distortion of you.

We grew cold.
Forehead swaddled in gauze, expanded. Somewhere—

there were those Bullets. Havocing bone and vessels. Vortexed
into cavity, they were lodged. *Brain Bullet, Brain Bullet*, I called, but

it did no good. We could not needle them out. At our white

columned porch and blue bulleted door I saw your last rush of air, last
shock, pulling in, pulling in. What were you pulling in?

REMEMBER THIS

When you were born, I peered at
you from our parents' bed, on the

wide mattressed field you were
alone, blue blanketed, barely

any wisps of hair. I studied you there,
your slight squirms, the smallest penny

slit eyes. I held you and did not pinch
or squeeze. I carried you toward me.

When I was fourteen and you were ten,
and we were still shaped raw, soft enough

to squish between teeth and jaw. Our fleshy
limbs browned by summer sun. Too hot to

eat until nightfall, mother ordered at the
sandwich shop counter. We watched a man gazelle

over the counter. Robbery in progress. Mother
ducked! I ducked! But you stood static — transfixed

by the gleam of gun, your legs were steeled
in place, but I grabbed hold and pulled and pulled

Remember how I pulled you in, toward me.
Remember how I once kept you safe.

THE WRECKAGE

We wait for word of Brother.

Doctor's words. Someone says, *Brain Dead* and we wait
    again, for his passing

    into the next world.

My throat is paralyzed, strung
    dry and tight. Night descends,
into morning, opens into a blurred afternoon. Then the pronouncement.

    Grandmother must be told;
she tastes those words and

    howls, punctures morning clouds. Desert blooms—
grief.

    Her walnut skin sags, dampens. I see now—how much we carry within

    us,

all the liquid we keep, but

    I want only to be bone. So I tell the hawks to eat me clean, marrow and
    all. Turn me

to carcass, leave no fat or tenderness behind because

    when I return—from hospital, without you, I can't eat or sleep. Fearing
    the aperture

of loss, I bite my lip tight, bloody it good. Until finally,
    I come undone. I am an ocean, a sea
                surge —that floods and floods,

    curling my knees to chest I blanket myself. Hold on

    tight, to your empty bed, and still

I cyclone.

    Look into my eye, this viscous core,
    see how I pain for you. These heaves
    leave me wrecked. Track me
    by satellite, find me among
    the burnt and spent.

I AM SORRY FOR YOUR LOSS

I am sorry for your loss, someone says.
Those words crack the sky open, a ripe burnt
hurt; I tally death, my throat marked sore with an X for
Brother, Uncles, Sisters, Grandfathers, 18 unratified treaties.

Those words crack the sky open, a ripe burnt
line forms. Something seems to be missing here—
Brother, Uncles, Sisters, Grandfathers, 18 unratified treaties.
I always pack Brother's death certificate.

Line forms. Something seems to be missing here—
Under Brother's Ethnicity write: Cahuilla, Luiseño.
I always pack Brother's death certificate
in my broken suitcase, the one that doesn't stand straight.

Under Brother's Ethnicity write: Cahuilla, Luiseño.
Nothing fits right in those boxes so I write about
my broken suitcase, the one that doesn't stand straight.
Pushing it, I refuse to cede to the weight, remembering extermination.

Nothing fits right in those boxes so I write about
lingering over Sunday morning oranges, thump of break-dancers.
Pushing it, I refuse to cede to the weight, remembering extermination,
canyon road, the steady shake of rattle, Grandmother's soft lilt,

lingering over Sunday morning oranges, the thump of a break, the dancing;
I sing into a tiny cry, the business of mourning.
Canyon road, the steady shake of rattle, Grandmother's soft lilt.
I crave Brother's posole, something to feed me warm.

I sing into a tiny cry, the everyday business of mourning.
A simple ritual of story and ash makes me
crave Brother's posole, something to feed me warm.
I am sorry for your loss, someone says.

BROTHER AND I

Two Ghost Fish

Lake Tahoe, river stream. Eye
of summer. Father stops the car

    so we can descend into the run of
    of water, bigger than a lick. Sunned limbs

slip between liquid and rock,
toes curl in search of pebbled bed, something

    to keep us upright—Brother and I are twinned
    fish, darker than the weathered stones
        we climb over.

Brother, always the more adventurous,

grins, sets out the rougher

    way, swims north. I return
    to the bank that sprouts green grass.

      This is how it will always be: One of us
      leaving the other, but never
        meaning to. Stretching—
          our ancestral cord to the break.

AT THE HOUSE
Evidence

Double the pain into
a helix, then smash it
until it dulls regret. Learn to
distrust the night, distrust muscled
voices, distrust dark SUVs,
the unknown. Fold
what has been left:
a dozen or so soft black
shirts, sheets of paperwork,
faxes, phone numbers,
account statements, business cards.

Create to-do lists: feed yourself—
for a month of his last meal.
Break down when the bowl
empties. Break bowl, break
skin to get at the hunger—an arterial pull
slips through and cuts the spine.

Bills—Write *Deceased*,
write it until you think
you are writing *Diseased*.
Start to imagine this your truth.

A few striped collared shirts,
Never, or
barely worn.
Size 13 shoes.
One pigtailed crying child,
one infant,

one boy
who wants to be a man,
and refuses to cry.

THOSE WHO SPEAK TO
TREES REMEMBER

Trees have ancestors, a lineage, a history. Father tells Brother and me
    as he waters his hybrids.
        Mother coos to citrus leaves and

reminds us of the canyon and desert
    in us, the Indian and Mexican
        of us, how we are grafted like our citrus trees

that drop grapefruits to roof, then tumble to ground,
    their skin splits—and jeweled flesh glistens gold beneath
        white membrane, tiny sour tears. Brother was once

afraid of those sounds, the way the yellow spheres
    rolled from roof to ground. Splats of grapefruits made him
        fear sleep in his own room. We used to climb past

the tangelo tree, past bright pebbled skin to reach
    garage roof where we played war with neighborhood kids,
        throwing dropped fruit at each other. In the lazy heat of summer,

we soured with sweat and dirt, licked trails of ripe juice from our hands.
    Brother's friends remember him and our trees, the sweetness of our
        lemons. Now when his friends visit, even a year after his death,

they sit in the backyard of our parents' house, drink beer, talk
    to the orange trees and listen to falling globes of citrus. I listen to the
        rustle of leaves, the way fruit sings of Brother,
            an echo in the wind.

THE SWEET IN THE BITTER
Inland Empire

Brother is dying. Every night after that night I taste his after
death breath. I chase a pinhole light, inverted image:
Before gunshot heart and Bullet. When Father is
sweet citrus, a tree-lined orange grove, feeding us orange

globed stories. There is the Rialto packing plant and we run
our fingers against Grandfather's old Chevy, scent of citrus trees in our
grasp. Before this there was something else and we remember that too.
Father takes me to Grandmother's childhood home — San Timoteo Canyon.

Too much brush and fence to get at. This house — this is what we mean
when talk of the ranch. It is more than a note in a local history
book where we remain unnamed. We point to sepia photos,
fingertip of lives. Father becomes a shrug; Brother is always on his way,

except now the road curves and curves away from
home. Brother knew that Mother bloomed me
in a sweatshop, witness to steaming machines and
warm muscle, the exhaust of brown women, a salty

scent still clings to the roots of my hair, even after
years of sleeping between the pages of books.
Mother always says: throw the first punch. But now
Bullet voices violence, fields fallow in the sun, then turn

concrete, singing dollar promises. In one hand I weigh
witness and in the other, a perfect citrus sphere. Sometimes
it's hard to distinguish the sweet from the bitter, either way
I always spit out the pith, but Father eats that too. Father insists

we must not juice our navels, we must peel and eat
them whole. Do you remember this Brother? How I savor
the apex, the second fruit for last. If you asked,
I'd save it for you, that twinned fruit.

ONE YEAR MEMORIAL

One year after, and we look to the blue
        cataract sky. We are so heavy—
                we let wetness trickle
                    to skin, let it open
                        on to us, want it to give back
                            a little of what it has taken.

For Brother we hold a hundred white balloons.

In this California desert
      we worry little about seagulls or sea
          turtles filling their mouths
              with our balloons—our hunger,
            our longing. Because here,
              the ocean is a mouthed
                    wish, and the only beach is our cracked
                      concrete porches, where we look out
                    into a sea of brown nubbed grass.

For Brother we cling to globed helium.

Your daughter tracks her balloon,
        sole pink globe, from kid palm, to stiff
           branched palm tree—to cloud. One year
              after, and this is easy—it's just a balloon
              she's letting go.

For Brother, we release a hundred white balloons, we release, release—

My hand releases—opens

to rain. I want to believe in something—I am ready
to be bathed by sun, but it remains buried in the gloom.
I search the clearing for helium light—weightlessness.
We are always searching—the bravest, reddest
part of ourselves for some sign
of Brother.

MIDNIGHT MEMORIAL

2011

We mark the year, mark the night of our stolen
breath by crowding up against each other to
watch your face—tilted smile projected on
paint peeled garage. We inhale the moon,
suck in the clouds, try to satiate the desert
of our bodies that are always fumbling
at loss. Like Brother, stars are such distant
luminous spheres. One photo after another:
Brother in pool with children clinging to him,
Brother between parents at zoo, Brother on his
boat, and Brother in his Riviera driving away.
Is this what makes a life? I dampen
the grass, the concrete. I become a river,
my most natural self, a migration—this new
me, all the rocky bits of grief undammed.

Brother's children leave as night darkens, chills
bodies, music slows and our wetness continues
to spill out, lakes our eyes, the soil. How bright
we burst with memory, our hurt so radiant
we turn firelight, expose where we come undone.

The next day your Daughter examines the photos
from the night before. She's seven and says
she sees you in the pit, in the burnt wood
that spits flame. A flame we kept alive,
all night—for you. The smoky hisses spoke
your name. It whirled so raw.
She sees you in our oxygenated memory;
she sees you the way I want to see you.

FLIGHT

I was once unafraid to open doors, I flung them wide, cast my arm out into
the wild of city, but then I opened that door. Brother, there was once

six bullets, two men and they came for you—hunted you. I can't make out
their faces, they hide in the weathered night. Their identity—uncertain.

Faces and names slippery beneath the spine and sap of nopales.
In the rain, I can see no stars, no bright mass of plasma, my sky is all brown

pupil and white sclera. Bullet comes quick, my brain liquid. I want us to fly,
like the old ones, whose arms became wings and muscled flight. I want

to meet on the North Mountain, at that cupped arrow, to nest above
the wreckage. But we are so mortal, and there is little magic left

in this world. Long ago, we were birthed from a people named after Pain, now
those words feel right when Brain Bullet is so final—

But I survive—to breathe ghost and speak phantom. Every night I wait for my
wings, for prickly feathers to sprout

from my shoulder blades, wait for sharpness to break flesh—leaving,
my arms vestigial, leaving me, unafraid to fly.

BULLET TEACHES

WHAT BULLET TEACHES

I learn to speak in metaphor,
name your murder
Bullet. Call fear
        my starless night, red ocean.

Without you
I want to knife
the writer out of me—
I imagined you
        dead many times before,

for the good of story,
to warm my hands
on grief's heat. But on that endless night—
I am too human.
        There is no saving you
from rain-slicked men.

I constrict,
see only blue
door, my own cells fighting,
neurons at war. Brain turns sloppy. In your brain—Bullet
        Chest—
      Bullet, Groin—Bullet.

      On our porch I reach your
      body still
flushed with heat. I want to touch your shiver
lips, the flutter of your moth mouth, to tender
      the hurt. But fear has found

my fingers and your
brain cannot
speak.

Sometimes I only want to remember
the rain.

ENG 267: NATIVE AMERICAN LITERATURE

Spring Quarter 2020 / T' & Th 1:30 pm-3:50 pm
Instructor: Casandra López
Prerequisite: ENGL&101

This course will focus on selected works by Native writers.
We will examine poetry, non-fiction and fiction by
seminal authors like Leslie Marmon Silko as well as
exciting contemporary authors such as Tommy Orange
and Layli Long Soldier. We will discuss what these texts
teach us about what it means to be human, what it means
to be from a place, and how to be a good relative.

OPEN THE DOOR

Eyewitness

Ear, mouth, and hands become:
Witness. I'm all instinct. Arms and legs propelling

on their own, shutting door. There is a ringing inside
me. Bullet's rapid breath a thick wave I must escape.

Brother's mouth gurgles; I touch his flutter lips, his face still
penny warm. There is a buzz of black. Do you hear me?

Brother, is this what it sounds like for you? Where are
my screams? I speak

in a neighbor language. Father's fingers are fish,
drowning. They cannot dial a phone. Instead

Father searches for shotgun. In this house,
a siren's mouth of blue, red, and white light, the howls break

the buzz. Your baby's mother is a wail, she leans on a chair,
the wall, her bones melting, she is letting herself slip

into the current. There is a wetness here, all the rain. Cop bends
to Brother, slaps his face and asks: *Who did this to you?* We must fill

the bathtub with questions, let it run, spill over the edges, into the
ocean. Bird of paradise murmurs, my throat crackles nonsense,

so many questions. Even when night comes,
again. We must open the door. I don't always remember,

but my body does. My pinpricked follicles soldier up, throat locks, the
hurricane I push down, legs want to run from an invisible Bullet's drone.

Shhhh in my dreams, there are always doors.
In my dreams, they come. And I clip through the wild waters, mapping

the world. Know each exit, which windows break, where we break, still Bullet
catches us cold. I want to be a thick-shelled mollusk, clam up tight. Is that

Brother? His lumpy neck? His voice is caught in the veins of the orange trees.
Every day I open that door and think I am living someone else's life.

DEAR BRAIN BULLET

Because of you, we danger into feralness,

      open our mouths wide —
            speak to the dead.
We think Bullet
         might be calling   our name, we might

also belong to the dead. How else do we speak

        so clearly to them?

Bullet, because of you we clean —

        the blood from porch,
Brother's copper red scent.   We clean   and clean,

        but can't rid ourselves of the taste

of metal to tongue. Still — we try to patch the gape

      in the door, fill it

    with density.   Memory becomes

        archeology. We search for lost

city because of you, always moving,   wandering

                    from room   to room,

ruin   to ruin   speaking   with shadow
                    mouths to specters—
We are a rough   run of pain
                    we cannot rid   ourselves of

even when we spit   and curse
                              your name.

We upchuck
              on anger.   Let loose

the thick-neck guard   dogs, all teeth snarl.

Bullet, because of you, we animal

                  our wounds, lick them
clean,   taking needle

                  to fissures,   stitching,
wanting to mend   hurt into   aperture,

                  a pinhole star of clarity. But sometimes

there is no   quieting the wind   of rupture,

            we break   scabbed blood

              becoming what we could not imagine.

THE FIRST 48

I marathon A&E's *The First 48,*
      but this is no race. There is no finish line, no victory

here. It's rough course, lots of stumble and blood-caked knees that break
      fresh to liquid. I take comfort

in television, even as my screen fills with brown bodies
      so like Brother's—done made dead.

      After Bullet night
I promise to never turn away from the rib of the left behind,
      the long scope of loss. But I watch in mute. To mute

grief's steady sting, the pulse of regret. Their guttural cries echo here,
      in chest, in the capital

of heart, where I've rooted Brother, so he grows from muscle to memory to
      story. When Nephew enters, I'm fast to change

channel, wanting to save him from death, the way I couldn't save
      him from son-pain.

Sometimes we have to mouth-knuckle the red of pain to white, so not to unfurl
      to a scream. I watch for clues—with the certainty

of the unsolved, forever. The weight of X heavier than
      anything we carry. X of fear, X of terror, wraps itself

into an equation we look for city to solve, each face a possibility, a mutation
      of the unknown.

The equation of self always
ends in Grief, a syllable too small to contain
        what it must. Our First 48 has passed, and still

we have X, so I speak to the television,
        to Miami's and Baltimore's detectives more than

anyone working Brother's case. I see myself in the blurred-out shaky face of

        witness. And I try to imagine Bullet being questioned.
Some resolution. How our episode would end.

AN UNKNOWN

For Jim Thorpe (Wa-Tho-Huk | Bright Path) and Brother

Jim was always running away from schools, and who knows
what else. One of the greatest athletes in the world is born

in what is called Indian Territory, but on this continent isn't it all.
He is a Bright Path, a Mark of Lightning. At nine, his twin dies in Indian

Agency school and Jim believes brother gives him
his strength — —a muscled quickness. So much death. Is that what

keeps him running? And what about me and my own ghost
twin Brother? How big he grows, story tries to fill in

that loss, my own mark. I am no athlete, but I'm always
running from something—a city I feared would eat

me whole. Instead it came for Brother—such teeth the night
has. I wonder if Jim was at his brother's side when he died

of pneumonia or was he somewhere running. Does he mean to never
leave, promise not to, and then still leave? I want to never leave Brother's

side as he is moved from concrete: gurney: hospital bed.
I want to be lightning, nature's muscle that can crack

Bullet from gun. I want the stars in my palms, fire in my hands.
I want to hold Brother's warmth a bit longer, for his heart to thump

and thump and thump. For it to sing me the song I need
most. Jim Thorpe's son dies still filled with such want, longs for his father's

remains, for them to be returned to their homelands, for ash to find its place in their red earth. I keep Brother within me, next to

Grandmother's river valley and Grandfather's orange trees—sweet rind of history I cultivate even as I run.

WHAT BODY CAN BEAR

Because Cousin calls you Brother, she drove— —
Arizona to California, through fogged night and rain.

Highway is gray-eye shock. She found us

in hospital waiting room, our mouths numb.
Brother in ICU, chest split down
         center, your children tattooed above your

heart. Cousin said her goodbyes. Now there is something
growing within her. She tells me it's the lymph nodes,

such heavy cells, multiply
         —body might break
         her. I taste the thick of her words

and think of your name
         stretched across her back, in rays

of light and clouds. Cousin's newly inked flesh is a pain
she can bear.

I ask her: Do you remember

Baja summers, hot salt beaches, our sanded
hair, or Tahoe's green mountains, that quick stream,
         the rush nearly carrying Brother

away? Cousin says she remembers it all, each summer,
         a cell, budding into tumor.

FOR THOSE WHO DREAM OF THE DEAD

Night, a cavernous
center, turns me jealous of those
                    who dream

of the Dead. Aunt sees Grandfather, a small
man with cigarette in one hand and oxygen
                         tank in other.

Then there is Sister-In-Law and
Cousin who Brother visits. But he will not
                    come for me

even when I open
          all four chambers, the steady fist

of my love. I am left with

the hush of night, sleep coaxed
          by the faint beat of helicopter wings,
                         our city

bird hovering in dark sky, flashing light that is
          not Brother. In Cousin's vision
                         Brother arrives

in his big wheeled truck and
                    drops her off

at Grandmother's house. Cousin is chemo-brained,
          her own cells made enemy. She pleads

to Brother,
　　take me with you.

He refuses and she wakes to white
　　　　walls—her brain dissolving, thawing

body soft against
　　　　chair. I want to corral her trance into my arms
　　　　　　longing for the faintest

residue of his presence. I tell Cousin:

I will stay here with you as long
as you need to nurse this liquid dream.

Let me stay here

　　with you between

Brother's breath and
　　　　drugged treatment—Cousin wants to say if

　　her mouth
　　　　was not
　　　　　　floating
　　　　　　　　above her like
　　a moment she wants to suck
　　　　　　clean.

LAKE DAYS

San Bernardino Mountains

I say blood—that family vein,
but what I mean is: roots—those rough
organs, fibrous DNA.
Since Brother's Bullet night I keep

unearthing them, only to replant—water
and tend to what I can make flower. I eat
my fill of oranges and peaches from family
trees. I don't forget to sour my tongue

with lemons, while fingertips graze the bite
of birds of paradise. I remember lake days,
the ease of us as we became mountains,
the thick of green. Father and you cast out—

      your reels,   thin lines   floating
over water,   disappearing— Teaching
      your Son   and Daughter to cast.

I ask your children: What can we lure from water?
Do you remember—how to angle the hook,
from body to liquid to body. What did we catch
that day? Not one fish, but something so
slippery, we reel it in daily to not forget.

PIÑON MAN

Grandfather was a piñon
nut of a man, hard
to unshell,

made love difficult. But not
you, Brother, so easily I fall
into a spell,

finding a soft place to rest
my Brother-Death blues.
You loved

Grandfather as a lean limbed
brown boy. He took you
to the mountains,

a forest of oak and pine to feed
squirrels and birdwatch blue jays
and sparrows, leaving

behind a valley of asphalt, scrub
brush and our palm tree guarded
block. Grandfather

told stories that were more
imagination than fact, but maybe
there's some truth,

in his spin of words. Years later,
when Grandfather shriveled
small

from age, drink, and smoke,
you'd pick him up when he'd fallen
on porch,

or from bed, or on casino escalator
with a swift lift from your brambly
arms, inked

with tattoos and work, even as he rasped
at you to stop. But it's you Brother who leaves
us first

and I become one long cry
of your name. Grandfather shrinks
smaller, drinks more.

He becomes a rough rock of pain
I can fit in my hand. When Grandfather leaves,
we remember

how Brother was to take Grandfather's ashes
and spread then in that forest, among
the green branches

of younger days. That was before I knew
the heft of urn, the weight of
their remains.

THE DARKEST OF DESERTS

In an Albuquerque museum I find
Brother hidden in Eva Hesse's *Spectres*. I push
past the glass doors, trying to lose
myself, tame my bright red parts in her brush
of shadows, her blue gray swirls—the ghostly
apparitions of body and face. I want to drown,
in her ocean of smoggy flesh and line, but
the Salton Sea in me survives. I am all salt
lungs and shallow breath when Brother emerges
from the painting, covered in blooms
of algae, moss green meets brown skin.
I ask a skeletal figure on the canvas:
What might I see if Brother hadn't been taken?
What other phantoms hover here, in museums
of memory? Eva with her Brain Tumors
and you with your Brain Bullet.
She painted these at 24. At 24, you
fathered two children, a brick house.
Bullets had not pierced us then.
I, too, learned the difference between
gunshots and backfires. How to push
body against the rough, the solid—hide within
the crevice of light. Your love leaves
behind your coarse hands, the red brick house.
Your truck takes you, work takes you. You let
night take you. We learn to wait for the lip
of dawn. Four years later, the night
takes and takes—leaving ragged breath,
and us waiting, our throats shocked
closed from hands that turn bullets

brutal. Scared of what we paint gray,
consume in the dulls of aftermath; I wade
into the dusk of Eva's paintings, looking
for what we lost, for the whiteness
of parched bones to illuminate.

NEW LANGUAGE

A NEW LANGUAGE

My words are always
        collapsing

upon themselves, too tight
        in my mouth. I want a new
language. One with at least
        50 words for grief

and 50 words for love, so I can offer
        them to the living
who mourn the dead. I want

a language that understands
        sister-pain and heart-hurt. So
when I tell you Brother

is my hook of heart, you will see

the needle threading me to
        the others, numbered
men, women, and children
        of our grit spit city.

I want a language to tell you
        about 2010's
37th homicide. The unsolved:
        a man that my city turned

to number,
        sparking me

back to longer days when:
     Ocean is the mouth
of summer. Our shell fingers
     drive into sand, searching—we find

tiny silver sand crabs,
     we scoop and scoop till we bore and go
in search of tangy seaweed.

We are salted sun. How we brown
     to earth. Our warm flesh flowering.

In this new language our bones say,
     sun and *sea*, reminding us of an old
language our mouths have forgotten, but
     our marrow remembers.

REFUGIO BEACH

Brother piles sand on his pregnant girlfriend's belly.
On her sandy stomach I draw a belly button. Soon it will be dusk

and the last surfers in the distance will disappear
from this winter beach. We find ourselves here in a cove beneath

the sway of palm trees; we find ourselves here marked
by a place named beautiful in an old language that knows

the sound the creek makes as it flows into the Pacific; we find
ourselves here as family, me on vacation from college and them

on vacation from a grit city, a rough necked inland place of splintering
concrete. Soon, but not yet, First Son will be born,

face brown and smooth as a well washed stone. I try to catch
a wave—this moment with my feet, don't want it to go because

I want more of this, to wolf down a place, the blue
inside of me. Hide in the slope of this crescent

beach, far away from Bullet. We can keep
our secrets here, in the tar that stains our feet black.

We are not a delicate people, don't mind the stain
of ocean. The tide will rise with the moon

but I am not ready to leave; toes curling against sand. Later we fall
asleep to waves but awaken

to the rude sounds of the metro link reminding us this
refuge is only temporary.

YOUR NAME

A Diamond Stolen from Our Mouths

Someone took it, swallowed it whole. Stole,
a diamond from our mouths —

At the hospital you were hidden, cloaked
white curtains, pseudonymed. Your Son
thinks you are a superhero, doesn't believe —

Nurses typed out: D A V I D   D O E
plastic to wrist, you are renamed.

They said it was for your protection. How unsafe
the hospital felt, this world.

We are told in the afterlife our ancestors
will know our name — sometimes I believe.

We hid your assisted breath, your gun shot body,
We hid our shakes in clutched hands.

Metal and machinery bound

D A V I D   D O E,

an investigation number,
a patient, a body, but not Brother.

I wanted
    to not have answered the door, to not have closed it;
    to have lied, I wanted to blame instincts — fear. I wanted to give

you my lungs, my heart, my frenetic caged brain. Anything. To take
your place. Impossible—

I tried singing you on, into

the other world. But I wasn't taught,

how throat should unravel into ancient
map, larynx branching into sky and trachea land.

Blood vessels spiriting you along. *You will not get
lost—*
Instead, I held you tightly, weaving lifeline to
lifeline. And
traced the curve of a J on the back of your thick
hand.

WHERE CEMENT SPLITS

Here is where you died.
I could be pointing
           at my center. But I mean

family porch. The smallest fractures splitting
           cement.

           Two white pillars stand

guard over Mother's cat decorations
           and blooms

           of flowers—Aloe vera ready to split
open, honeyed
           salve. Children's toys, scooters, and bikes
worn
           to metallic bone from years of play.

           Here is where

I choked on sister-hope, wanting
           one last taste of sweetness before
Bullet.

           Is this the call

Brother-friend
           hears when he comes to talk

to you and drink beer, slipping into high school

days

of wearing your clothes, 3 sizes too big?

He sips from can, says he knows it's you

because   sometimes you give shitty advice.

There is a choir

of hummingbirds who return here

reminding me of the way my

veins   hum your name.

THIS DISTANCE

Santa Fe

I leave one desert for another, but I'm no
Indian scout, just someone trying to quiet the ache
I reach for when the night turns me into vibration
that cannot reach the 800 miles or so between

here and there. At sunset I watch birds chase
other birds, one leafed branch to another.
African grass growing in New Mexico soil,
fans in their wake, horse hair swaying. A fat bird

swooshes past me and caws. I want their language,
want to send a message to the messy sky
with brushed stroked clouds because somewhere
out there is Brother. Somewhere out there an owl

hoots his name. But tonight I refuse to hear it as death,
to remember Brother as night prey, instead I look
for the owl hoping to salvage a prayer from its hooked
beak but only see an orange bibbed bird screeching

past me. Brother never came to visit me in this place.
He never saw this grass move in tiny waves
yet he saw so much more than me, everything
I turned away from. A street number tattooed to arm,

stained bones and breath, and finally Bullet
death. He spoke those streets, with calm tongue
and hustle heart. I wonder if he ever imagined me
here, my brown body in another brown land.

ECLIPSE

Albuquerque 2012

Brother is my eclipse. The perfect
                alignment, one body covering
another. I wish my body more fierce, a shield
                to cover for Brother on Bullet night. My one great

regret eating at my brain. I'm becoming unfleshed. Investigate this:
                How do I walk around alive when there is all

of this consuming me? Can I name Bullet
                moon or is death the moon? What is it that leaves
the stain of fire behind? Eclipse

glasses perch on my nose. Halo of orange. Halo of red. I try to see into the sky,
                where Brother is said to be, even as the body
I knew as his was made into particles.

                There was no moon on Bullet
night, but maybe that is only memory.
                I remember the rain, the darkness,
my fear. The next day I saw no sun, I ate
                the clouds, the dampness soaked into my boots.
The moon had nothing to cover, but we were
                eclipsed.

Bullet or maybe moon left me with a stain of fire. My lament,
                a badge, follows me everywhere I go. Sometimes the
                blaze

is fury. Sometimes it is a soft sorrow. I look to the sky and I see it all
                burning.

SUDDENLY IT COMES AND

All of the poets
        are writing
           about the eclipse
               of moths

                  that thicken
                     our vision, their dust flesh
                        and wisps of wings.
But I still write
        Brother.

            And taste his absence,
                death my own moon
                    shadow, sending slices
                  of grief I suck
                 and spit,
turning me
        delicate
          as damp newspaper I use to ghost-
                 swat recollections.

A flutter of moths dance,
        mill above me,
           chasing
             light and warm night.
                I remember: Brother
born
    at the break
        of April.

Born of grit and meadow,
            brown as a ruddy nut—skin
            that spoke
            of our desert
                        blood.

Moths swarm. Poets catch them—

        bloated New Mexican bugs—

        between fingers, against alcohol-

                soaked tongues, mouths filling

                        with earthy cinder.

A Diné poet tells me
        an old story. Why she won't touch them.

                She was taught

                about a madness,

                        shivering bodies and
                        fire.

        But April death is insistent,
                nature comes
                        silently,

each tiny carcass
        a downed plane

littering

the horizon.

Despite the warning

I scoop up stiff-bodied

moths with bare

hands, examine

their thin scales, marvel

at lightness. I no longer want

to be afraid.

BIOLOGICAL

I want to tell him that since Brother-Death
I haven't been the same, but he already knows,

the way my mollusk shell cracks beneath
the slightest thumb pressure. Underneath

exoskeleton—I'm all ache and bruise, so biological.
He's turned me into the dampest beach

sand, a million soft granules. He is a wave
and ocean right at my ear. Saltation—

wind—suspension—carried—particle by particle
toward him. So exposed it is to be undeclared and

unnamed—we a wild beach with no lifeguard in sight.

IN THIS DESERT

I'm always finding grit between
my teeth. The smallest pebbles upswept

into languid tongue. The desert is so close—tiny
granules make bright constellations—such sharp

light. But then he enters and sweeps away the mountains
of minuscule. Survivalists say you should suck

on a pebble to stave off thirst. Even though
I wasn't taught much, I know they learned it from

the old ones. I hide pebbles in the bed as a test, see
if he notices the way they badger flesh—I want him

to mouth them, back to me, remind me that I'm 78%
water and even the desert sometimes rains. My brown

thighs hum from the trace of his fingertips. I feel soft
about what his almost white hands find there,

want to welcome him in, but instead I wonder if I can
love someone who can never know what I've lost.

What I really want to ask is: Can I love after that blood
stain I sometimes rub raw? I'm always trying to get at

that hurt. I ask him if he can taste my bitter, and watch
his face for signs of puckering. Will he grow tired of my sour?

The way I serve melancholy for dinner. I'm always inviting ghost
guests to the table; I ask him to set a plate for Brother,

another for Uncle and Grandfather, make way for the family
tree, so I can dig a hole in the living

room and plant a nopal, let him find the thorns, as we wait
for it to fruit, so there might be a little sweetness as we bite history.

CONTINENT OF DESIRE

We arrive on this continent
     of desire,

no borders in sight. Quick to turn
     ungoverned, we talk
about territories
        dissolving.

How young to feel unwrapped,
     the whole of us
so new to each other, my brown

against
     his — not brown
body.   Outside
there is so much mass. A galaxy
     of other.

Close your eyes,
     I tell him, let's hide beneath
        this thin
           skin, a veil against

the sunlight or is it the moonlight? The distant
     stars are making a sound

we have no words for. On the other side
     of the window dust
        colored birds sing
migration   songs, fluttering
     on boney branches. I request

another tune,
        one that doesn't remind me
of my travels. I wonder
        if he sees
how haunted I am, all of the dead

        I whisper to, all the names
I want etched   into my flesh,
                a soft
terrain to lay
                down
for those I fear
                forgetting.

This is the way
        the dead and I
will grow old together.

        There is a map here, somewhere

and I, a confused cartographer
        adding to it, and expecting
him to follow.   Out there —
        across the deserts
and mountains, and
        thin lined boundaries is
my other life:

        A civilization
                of memory, my sweet city
of despair, where the young are not
        young for long. I pull him close,
wanting to feed him

        memories of my dearest,
    my Bullet-
    stolen
    sibling,

who I can only write as:

    Brother.

So frequently
    I speak of longing,
a language weighted with
    impossibility,

but right now I say:
        remember this moment—
how we mouth
            hunger,
        remember the way we
map ourselves anew.

REMAINS

WHAT REMAINS

Baja summers. Mother washed us in plastic tubs,
bathed us in gray salt light. We rushed down,
rocky hill. Found the tiniest octopus and kept it
in a toy castle. Lit fireworks in Coke bottles.
We were combustible —

Now we keep you inside, boxed and urned. We keep you
inside the silver and slick of us. But
what about Bullet lodged in body? Do we keep
Bullet next to mantel or flesh?

At the beach, you woke early, gravitated to the low
tides. The night before, slippery grunions whispered
and circused across our feet. Following your path,
I shivered and sidestepped a speared stingray inking
sand, blooms of jellyfish. I searched

for your thin sunned brown back — but only saw the Sea
of Cortez. You are ash, chemicals compounded. You hide in
my glass pendant, sparkle green and blue, glint gold — transformed.
Five pounds of specks remain. Shouldn't there be more?

Arizona — endless white sky, each grain of sand,
an ember. Hot enough to burn — vaporize bone.
We squint at the sun's glare, at the glimmer of reservoir.
I am shored while you boat out and smile. Water carries you
away. I wish I could swim myself to you, fin out for one last look
as your broad back becomes a brown speck, becomes ash — a distant star.

SOMEONE

Drove across
     the street over the curb, over
slick blades of grass and broke
          our chain-link fence.
She was a smash of anger and drink.

I think a part of her was
broken, the way we have been broken since

Brother died. It's a part that hurts
on a night hushed
dull except   for a woman screaming.

     The woman tries
to run over
     a man, someone who did her wrong.

A different man did us wrong.
Ordered you dead
       on a different night.

But I know this feeling—

A wide–open–gash of gut
that causes this woman to
crash into cars,
crash into fence,
crash into our playground,
and into our sleep.

Planks of wood topple, a small child's
playhouse ready to tumble. We have
already been left
        unsteady.
No quick fix
for the broken.   Hinges unscrewed,
wood chopped and
        nails collected.

Father asks: What can we salvage?

He sits here, beneath the sun,
      tear hunched, canyon calling
Brother's name, waiting for a response.
Father says: The fence needs mending,
dirt dug. His shovel breaks
    spring ground.

SUN RECEDING INTO EARTH

Driving, the sun is too beautiful to turn away
from. But then the air turns foul. Scientists blame
the dead bubbling from a brackish body

of water, they blame rotten fish, and rogue
winds stirring up the Salton Sea. Everyone rolls up
windows to protect their lungs, but we still can't escape

the stench of it, reminding us of what hides
in the smallest part of ourselves. I remember the dead.
Stories of Grandfather's old boat, how he fished for

corvina and sargo in that sea. *Good lookin' fish,*
he'd say. And when they hooked a tilapia, they gave it
away. I ask myself if these are names of fish or memories

of people unafraid of the sun's brute strength. Grandmother
names each person who fished on *Leaky Lena,* ending
their names in a sigh, most of them gone now too.

Years before salt decayed trailers, before fish-stink and waves
of botulism, grandparents would escape to Bombay Beach
from town when they tired of city ways. These days algae

blooms and scientists warn—*only tilapia will survive,*
until they won't. West of the sea-funk we think we are safe
from miles of fish and bird bones ground white to

sand. Death so close you can crunch the spines and heads
of sun washed fish beneath feet. On a day like this, with so much
certainty in the sky and death's scent following me everywhere,

I want to speed into it, shed my own murky skin, to reveal the red
glow that hollows through my bones. Here, we yearn to catch what's always
out of reach, a luminescence, that beckons our dead to the surface.

SOMETIMES

When he speaks of *love*, I think of conquest,
        cottonwood trees and years of river,
chiseling away at time. Show me how the bold
        believe. Because all I can think about is
what he will take and what I can give.
        Sometimes I want to bend—to the distance,
those great states—lines we draw on maps,
        and between us. I would like to tell him,
how he makes me feel darker—without making him feel—whiter.
        A simple statement from the once hunted;
my body a trumpet. I want to cup his mouth with my hands, showing
        him how to purse his lips to play ancient
instrument. Then I will ask: Did you see the thread
        of desert, the way it steals the moon from the night?
Listen again, to the way brass valves rise in my chest, between
        the rattle of gourds, such an old cadence. That part
of me always singing about the dead—little ghost songs
        of longing. I used to think it was about showing him
where I am from, but now I think I must make
        him feel it—the prick of green succulents, and how
Mother's house shakes from Brother's bass,
        that thump of stereo that rattles through our teeth.

MOUTHED MEMORY

They say the sky is beautiful here,

       the way New Mexico sun exposes the light
              blue days. The sky always beckoning

artists. I know one, who obsessively paints
              a triangle of windowed sky. A prisoner to
              beauty, she hunches
                 over table, fingers turning

her black pants to a hue of blue. She clocks

       daylight with studies of color. Her fingers must
              know there is some poetry here in these
       names:

cerulean, celeste, turquoise, azure, because a morning

       song murmurs in the thin bristles of her paint brush,
              searching for photographic precision.

In Santa Fe another painter tells me,

       Look at those clouds—amazing. Her sunglassed
              eyes linger, then shaking her head she says,

some artist is gonna fuck it up.

       I concede to this beauty, but prefer the night sky and sunset
              anticipation, darkness cloaking my orbiting
              path away from

home, but know this feeling, the poems I can't get right,

   one for Mother, one for Father, all that Brother-Death
     I can't tether to jaw. I'm reminded of all
     I get wrong. Today I can't stop

but wonder what he sees in this—

   sky. When he admitted he loved
     the "West" and cowboys I thought him silly,

boyish—and white. I thought of history. Settlers

   looking for a kind of independence in this desert,
     much like him driving into Santa Fe, becoming

that Neil Young song. I thought of the distance between,

   Albuquerque and Santa Fe—a memorized lyric,
     how distance is always more than geography.
     I thought

of my desert with its concrete sky, all that gravel and

   California smog, my desert of grief, never leaving me
     me lonely. Desert of succulents, canyon rock

creeks and chain-linked fences. I thought how when it was good

   I wanted him to love my desert too, because on a clear day you
     can see the North Mountain; how it breathes
     through me.

BONE MAP

He says nothing of my leaving, but I am
always the most willing to shock cold this desert

muscle—steady the pulse of the right and left ventricle. My teeth rattle off
in the distance, searching for their way back to sand the color of

my palms, or anything to hold on to. I like to speak in *remember whens,*
when his warm breath did not turn so quickly to vapor,

but settled in the nape of neck. For him I exposed
my vertebrae, thirty-three curved pieces, a bone

map for his fingers. I wanted him to trace it, from pelvis up
to the sky because it's there, where there used to be only room for ghosts.

I used to be a welcome for him, an audience for all
his theories. Now I need a way back. I begin with curved clavicle, trying

to connect it to scapula, ordering my bones into a path, but I am too lost
and must look to the stars where Brother lives with the old

ones whom I trust to navigate me through the seasons, fall to
summer, back to fall, by the thirteen moons. They say the Milky

Way is just kicked up dust. They say to learn the stars by stories—sisters,
brothers, hunters and sheep—where all the lonely go. Will I remember

him only as a story, the time it seemed like we were our own constellation,
a star pattern, worthy of charting, worthy of theory. I am an orbit

of loss. Our bodies so distant. Is this why I fear the boundless
sky, a celestial void? The old ones know *theory* is just another way

to say *story*. But what about what he keeps quiet? How do I track
silence? Tell me anything, story or theory, something

I can follow and I will tell him: All the lost parts of me
are out there looking for the fixed, a grid to hold up hope.

PEELED FRUIT

This is a sibling story. First Son a clone,
        grafted from your wide acorn
                face. It's easy to mistake
his face for yours, Brother.
            I hand him first segment of orange, then   split
              another piece for Daughter, carefully   peeling
                                        away

membrane for Second Son.
            He is a good eater,
        out of diapers now and knows

your name,   even if he can't remember how

            your burly chest housed
a soft rumble of praise.

Brother I want to tell you: I am learning to speak
            in two languages,   one on the page and one
            off,

like you
            I now have secrets.

Brother did you ever see Mother cry? My first time is
            at hospital. She is a fierce and bitter howl,
                    curling into a rounded
                            fist.

I try to dream of you, instead   a cold snap

                    comes, winter's bite we have been

                  warned about,

          but pushed away

into the folds of pillows.

        Now we must search

              for the ripe, slick liquid

                  hidden

                      in our oranges.

Father knifes   their skin

              in a spiral. This is how I feel sometimes,

              like skinless

              ripe fruit, so heavy.

Other days I blossom white, petals   reaching

          out into a green leaved tree.

WHEN I WAS A YOUNG GIRL

Mother once told me a story.
In this story a mother throws herself on to her son's
coffin, not wanting him

        to be lowered
        into the ground.

This mother soul sobs the way
only survivors can. A hunched
        rack of body, draping
                over slick coffin.

She is bones and lungs;
needs to be pulled   back and into arms.

        I find myself returning here

        often
        to this grieved need.

We had no coffin for Brother. Mother didn't cry into
his casket. Her howls were kept

        hidden that day,
        twined sharp
        against muscle.

Later they would break

free into porcelain sink while

Brother's body was at the

coroner's.

There were papers to be filed,
a body to be   dissected.

We try to right this—
purify the desecrated—turn
                his body to ash.

                We try to right this.
                We try and try
                to right this.
                And I write this—fearing no one else will.

I return here
to Mother's words
as they become
mine
                but I can never finish

writing a mother's loss—

Not when there are Mothers on TV. Mothers in newspapers.
Some made fragile, some made fierce

                by the theft of   child.

                Theft of gravel

       and shovel,
       theft of name
       theft of future
       theft of mother
       and father
       theft of sister
       and brother
       theft of friend
       and lover
       theft of names
some we will never know.

Who will hold these mothers up

               off of caskets, off of sinks, and
               into arms?

SISTER SONG

I am not much more than a promise of a song,
that Brother never asked me to sing, our forever song,

but the crack of streets is sometimes a prison.
It wasn't always this way, me swallowing a far song.

Once your neighbor friend chewed a lightbulb and didn't
cry. His child-mouth smiled, a glass cracked marred song,

close to lips. On the 4th of July you used to like to light
the streets on fire, we'd become bright—a North Star song.

These days I stay inside when there is too much noise,
shattered bottles or loud aerial dances; I become a scarred song

remembering Brother, a street number tattooed to your arm
you can't rub off. It inks my own, a tarred song,

that never feels clean. Once you trucked a load of fireworks across
borders. Mother forbid it, not wanting you to become a guarded song,

an imprisoned light. Sometimes I tire, all the singing, want to witness
the sky boom, flare and burn, want to hear you call me *Sister* again.

SECOND SON, BRIGHT STAR

We teach your son to say *Daddy*. Kiss
your portrait-face shaped by the lightest air

brushed strokes. White canvas and black paint is what
we can offer wanting baby, now toddler. I want to stop

time for you. Let you see him now,
your third child, Second Son. A late star

you once cupped in your arms with tired
eyes. How unfair life is that we grow

older and you stay the same, changing only
in memory, perhaps becoming softer,

a dry brush swirl. But I want none of that.
I want to give Second Son all—of you. Scalpel

each moment from my brain, placing it
on silver tray for him to examine. I will point

to that piece with your pyromaniac
tendencies, and tell of the rush of joy

on your face when you lit fireworks off
illegally into the sky, how bright we were

against the dull of night. You were always our light,
splitting the black sky. How we still burn for you.

4TH OF JULY

San Bernardino 2015

South of the freeway fireworks spit
out the whole of July.

Booms blare louder than backfires,
thundering into sky.

My friend says, no one cares if we burn
ourselves down here.

Past 30th we spark and catch fire
so easily.

We brittle as palm leaves; we dry as
brush and concrete.

Here on 10th, we prop up cannons on
poles of chain-link fences.

Here on 10th, dogs howl or cower as
fire hungry teens slow

cars with their jolting limbs crashing into
each other in the center

of the street like this is the center
of the world.

I'm always leaving, but this still remains
the center of my world,

my sun center, hottest part of ache,
my core of joy. Sometimes

it is too much and I have to shield
my vision, where I pain

easily. This is the concrete, asphalt and
chain-link Brother and I grew from.

When Brother tattooed this street
into his arm Mother thought:

now he would never leave. This was partial
truth. This street, these numbers

had dug their way into his ruddy skin
since birth.

As a boy before cell phones chirped, buzzed, or
pinged he'd call to his friends

down the street with a high pitched animal whistle.
This is the way 10th sings

city, sings of lives undiagnosed of witness and
hurt. Even the dogs learn this tune.

It's been four years since Brother's murder,
and I ask myself:

When will I be post of post-traumatic?
Post guilt or post disturbance? When will

fireworks sound only like fireworks?
I try to enjoy Youngest Nephew's

face as Uncle wows him by lighting
fireworks, cracking open the night,

marking 10th with smoke and light.
Tonight I only see faces bright

with smiles and think nothing of
flag or country.

SOME BOYS

When Brother's First Son asked me
where it happened, where his father could not outrun

death, I tell him the truth, but feel heavy with the
weight of witness, a wild gunshot ricochets in my

throat. He wants to know if it happened in the back
yard where his father as a boy once raced behind orange

and sweet lemon trees, scrambling over warped
fences to escape BB gun games. Shoulders shot by other boys.

Brother was a big target. Tiny bullets pierced summer
skin but they smiled at the gunplay with those they called *brother*.

These easy pains heal clean. They are not the ones that mark
some boys. Boys that always carry those scars, even after

wounds are no longer circled red. Mother tells First Son not to
wear his hoodie over his head. Don't walk to the corner store alone.

Be back before the streetlights turn on, she says, just like she told
Brother as a boy. Are these the warnings Brother would have given his son,

knowing that sometimes it is not enough because some boys,
some brown boys are never just boys to some.

FOR THOSE WHO LEARN TO SEW SORROW

Let me mend this for you, I say to Niece,
let me sew our sorrow—stitch at what we
are left with, let me teach you, where we place
our fingers next to sliver of needle.
Let me show you a woman's strength, already
conjured forth from you at seven years old.
I see it, in your ghost cries for daddy,
in the way you hold counsel at brass urn.

I tell you, like Mother told me, when we
become blood pricked, we suck in the crimson
drop, take in the taste of metal to rough
nubbed tongue and continue, guiding fabric.
Our hands brown to desert, turn the ravaged
tender—our fingers winded memory.

ORANGES ARE NOT INDIGENOUS

to the place I call home,
not like we are. But when I am away
and Father sends a box
of oranges, I open it and breathe
in the scent of home.
It calls me back
even on the days when
Brother's voice grows quiet.
When Uncle packed up
Brother's clothes, I angered—
I wanted to keep alive Brother's
scent as long as possible.
When I dream regret, I press
my face into his chest—Brother's body
as big and brown as a bear, my nose resting
against his soft black shirt and inhale—
Our oranges begin to ripen
in December. We wait
for the branches to hang heavy
with the fruit before
a harvest as we also ripen—
with blood-loss. We grow and
release. This December ceremony. This death
date is sharp and sweet. Marked
on calendars and our bodies.
Marker of time. Marker of new
memories. Before Bullet,
Youngest Nephew was barely
formed, but now he helps me pick
lemons, pointing to the brightest

ones that are sometimes out of reach.
In April we celebrate Brother's birth
with the cars he loved.
His '67 Riviera is washed and detailed.
The rims cutting against the gaze
of the sun. Isn't this how you would
want it? Your First Son and Brother-Friend
cruising this city, your car dancing,
its body suspended by a rush
of tanked air. We are all suspended
in that between place
as the parking lot vibrates
bass. Spring comes and mint grows soft
and green from a leaking faucet in the
backyard. My face presses into
ground and I inhale—It grows
even when Brother's children do not visit
or I have been away. I need these reminders of
how we survive and still grow
so fiercely against the edges of this earth.

ACKNOWLEDGMENTS

I owe my deepest gratitude to my parents who have been a constant support. They have been the source of strength that I needed to complete this book. I appreciate all the direction and support I received from my professors and fellow students at the University of New Mexico. I wrote many of these poems during residencies with the Santa Fe Institute and School of Advanced Research. Some of the poems were in published in the chapbook, *Where Bullet Breaks*, which was edited by the wonder poet, Nickole Brown. I'm grateful for the encouragement of my friends and family, especially those from back home who have shared with me their memories of Brother and who still keep those memories alive. I'm especially appreciate all those who allowed me to write about them and saw I was writing from a place of love. This book is dedicated to Brother. I will also wish we had more time together.

The following poems appeared in the chapbook, *Where Bullet Breaks*, which was published by The Sequoyah National Research Center:

"Where Bullet Breaks" *Hobart*

"Open The Door: Eye Witness" *Grist*

"Where Cement Splits" *Bluestem*

"Those Who Speak to Trees Remember" *Orangelandia Anthology*

"Brother and I: Two Ghost Fish" *Kweli*

"What Bullet Teaches" *Malpais Review*

"What Body Can Bear" *Toe Good Poetry*

"For Those Who Dream of The Dead" *Malpais Review*

"A New Language" *Catamaran Literary Reader*

"The First 48" *Grist*

"Suddenly It Comes" *Cura*

"Eclipse: Albuquerque 2012" *Orange Monkey Publishing*

"The Darkest of Deserts" *California Journal Of Women Writers*

"An Unknown" *Huizache*

"Father Made Us," previously titled "Desert Deep" *The McNeese Review*

"One Year Memorial" *Hobart*

"10th St Porch: Investigation" The Acentos Review

The following poems first appeared in the following journals:

"In This Desert" *Bellingham Review*

"Sister Song" *Codex Journal*

"What Remains" *Sakura*

"This Distance" *Forth River*

"Sweet in The Bitter" and "Peeled Fruit" *Orangelandia Anthology*

"Some Boys" *Raven Chronicles*

"Mouthed Memory" *Pilgrimage Magazine*

"Evidence" "Sometimes" *Literary Orphans*

"Open The Door: Eye Witness," "The First 48," "Dear Brain Bullet" *Grist*

"Those Who Dream of The Dead,""Bone Map" "Sun Receding Into Earth" *Malpais Review*

"Where Cement Splits" *Bluestem*

"Piñon Man," "Continent of Desire" *Agave*

"Brother And I: Two Ghost Fish" *Kweli*

"Flight" *Hobart*

"For Those Who Sew Sorrow" *Labletter*

"Biological" *Más Tequila Review*

"Your Name: A Diamond" *Weber–The Contemporary West*

"Midnight Memorial" *San Pedro Review*

"The Wreckage" *200 New Mexico Poems*

"Refugio Beach" *World Literature Today*

"4th of July: San Bernardino 2015" *The Feminist Wire*

"When I was a Young Girl" *About Place Journal*
"Someone" *Dreginald*
"I'm Sorry Your Loss" *Anthropoid*
"Lake Days" *Red Ink*

ABOUT THE AUTHOR

CASANDRA LÓPEZ is a Chicana, Cahuilla, Luiseño, and Tongva writer raised in Southern California. A CantoMundo Fellow, López is a founding editor of the literary journal, *As/Us: A Space for Women of the World* and teaches at Northwest Indian College.